Hunting
Log Book

HUNTING SEASON

Fact & Fiction:
Records from my
hunts.

BOOKS WITH SOUL

Books With Soul
Somewhere in the desert, sea and forest.
www.bookswithsoul.com
∞
Books with Soul supports copyright for all authors.
Thank you for purchasing a copyrighted edition of this book.
First Edition 2018

ISBN-13 978-1-949325-35-5

Special thanks to all the hunters in my life; my brothers, uncles, Dad, cousins, nephews, neices and all the friends I grew up with.

This one's for you Dad.

**Inside this book
are the
hunting adventures
of**

_____

**I started recording my
hunting trips
& excursions on:**

_____

Life is a collection of moments

moments

-unknown

Hunting Season

Hunting Season

For generations, Hunting Season is a placemark in the year. A special time where countless hunters anxiously anticipate a season to call their own.

So highly covenanted, in most parts of the USA and the world, it is a season of its own.

Growing up in Western Pennsylvania, the rule was simple, absolutely nothing could be scheduled during this season. It was a golden rule. No family weddings, vacations or major events. And of course, the 'First Day of Buck', is naturally a school holiday.

Take time to record your hunting adventures and memories. Pass them down or just reflect on the stories. If you begin now, you will have the memories recorded and in 20 years, you'll be thankful you started this process.

Log the date, who you went with and what you hunted.

Record: weather, location, name of road, and anything that happened along the way (good or bad).

There's no season like Hunting Season.

Someday, you will have a collection of your memories and all the places you discovered hunting. Moments you took the time to write down in this log book. You'll never know who may benefit from your words and records or remember your journeys and hunting adventures.*

You are *A Collector of Memories.*
So, whether it is your 1st hunting experience, or your 500th, make a habit to take a few minutes when you return from each hunting excursion or trip, and write down a few details of the day.

Without doubt, you'll be thankful you have your Hunting Log.

My father, a magnificent man and avid hunter is sadly no longer with us on earth. But I'm sure he is still hunting-- in glorious fields and woods up above--every day. This year, my mother was giving an old desk of my fathers to my nephew Jake. When he took it back to Arkansas, he found an old journal hidden in the drawers.
A hunting journal. It was a priceless find. Words in my father's handwriting, and stories in his voice. No one knew he kept a hunter's log.
This discovery instills the mission of
Books with Soul.
Your Words, Your Pages.

Collect your memories.

Date: Hunting Location:

Hunters present:

Weather:

This is what happened:

Date: Hunting Location:

Hunters present:

Weather:

This is what happened:

Date: _____ Hunting Location: _____

Hunters present: _____

Weather: _____

This is what happened: _____

_____

_____

_____

_____

_____

_____

_____

_____

_____

_____

_____

_____

_____

A bad day hunting still beats a good day working.
-unknown

Date: Hunting Location:

Hunters present:

Weather:

This is what happened:

Date: Hunting Location:

Hunters present:

Weather:

This is what happened:

Date: Hunting Location:

Hunters present:

Weather:

This is what happened:

There is a passion for hunting something deeply implanted in the human breast. -Charles Dickens

Date: Hunting Location:

Hunters present:

Weather:

This is what happened:

Date: Hunting Location:

Hunters present:

Weather:

This is what happened:

Date: Hunting Location:

Hunters present:

Weather:

This is what happened:

Date: _____ Hunting Location: _____

Hunters present: _____

Weather: _____

This is what happened:
_____
_____
_____
_____
_____
_____
_____
_____
_____
_____
_____
_____
_____
_____
_____
_____

Date: _____ Hunting Location: _____

Hunters present: _____

Weather: _____

This is what happened: _____

_____

_____

_____

_____

_____

_____

_____

_____

_____

_____

_____

_____

_____

_____

_____

Date: _____ Hunting Location: _____

Hunters present: _____

Weather: _____

This is what happened: _____

_____

_____

_____

_____

_____

_____

_____

_____

_____

_____

_____

_____

_____

_____

_____

_____

_____

_____

I hunted with my father, he hunted with his father, he hunted with his father, he hunted with his father...

Date: _____ Hunting Location: _____

_____

Hunters present: _____

_____

Weather: _____

This is what happened: _____

_____

_____

_____

_____

_____

_____

_____

_____

_____

_____

_____

_____

_____

_____

_____

Date: Hunting Location:

Hunters present:

Weather:

This is what happened:

Date: Hunting Location:

Hunters present:

Weather:

This is what happened:

Date: _____ Hunting Location: _____

Hunters present: _____

Weather: _____

This is what happened: _____

_____

_____

_____

_____

_____

_____

_____

_____

_____

_____

_____

_____

_____

_____

_____

_____

_____

_____

Date: Hunting Location:

Hunters present:

Weather:

This is what happened:

Date: _____ Hunting Location: _____

Hunters present: _____

Weather: _____

This is what happened: _____

_____

_____

_____

_____

_____

_____

_____

_____

_____

_____

_____

_____

_____

Date: Hunting Location:

Hunters present:

Weather:

This is what happened:

There are fish tales
and
there are buck tales.

Date: Hunting Location:

Hunters present:

Weather:

This is what happened:

Date: _____ Hunting Location: _____

Hunters present: _____

Weather: _____

This is what happened: _____

_____

_____

_____

_____

_____

_____

_____

_____

_____

_____

_____

_____

_____

_____

_____

_____

Date: Hunting Location:

Hunters present:

Weather:

This is what happened:

Date: Hunting Location:

Hunters present:

Weather:

This is what happened:

Date: _____ Hunting Location: _____

Hunters present: _____

Weather: _____

This is what happened: _____

_____

_____

_____

_____

_____

_____

_____

_____

_____

_____

_____

_____

_____

_____

_____

_____

Of course it's a school holiday.

Date: Hunting Location:

Hunters present:

Weather:

This is what happened:

Date: _____ Hunting Location: _____

_____

Hunters present: _____

_____

Weather: _____

This is what happened: _____

_____

_____

_____

_____

_____

_____

_____

_____

_____

_____

_____

_____

_____

_____

_____

_____

Date: Hunting Location:

Hunters present:

Weather:

This is what happened:

Date: Hunting Location:

Hunters present:

Weather:

This is what happened:

Date: _____ Hunting Location: _____

Hunters present: _____

Weather: _____

This is what happened:

_____

_____

_____

_____

_____

_____

_____

_____

_____

_____

_____

_____

_____

_____

Look deep into nature and then you will understand everything.
Albert Einstein

Date: _____ Hunting Location: _____

Hunters present: _____

Weather: _____

This is what happened: _____

_____

_____

_____

_____

_____

_____

_____

_____

_____

_____

_____

_____

_____

_____

_____

_____

Date: Hunting Location:

Hunters present:

Weather:

This is what happened:

Date: Hunting Location:

Hunters present:

Weather:

This is what happened:

Date: Hunting Location:

Hunters present:

Weather:

This is what happened:

Date: _____ Hunting Location: _____

Hunters present: _____

Weather: _____

This is what happened: _____

_____

_____

_____

_____

_____

_____

_____

_____

_____

_____

_____

_____

_____

_____

_____

_____

_____

Date: _____ Hunting Location: _____

Hunters present: _____

Weather: _____

This is what happened: _____

_____

_____

_____

_____

_____

_____

_____

_____

_____

_____

_____

_____

_____

_____

Date: Hunting Location:

Hunters present:

Weather:

This is what happened:

If you're too busy to hunt
then you are
too busy. Slow down.

Date: Hunting Location:

Hunters present:

Weather:

This is what happened:

Date: Hunting Location:

Hunters present:

Weather:

This is what happened:

Date: _____ Hunting Location: _____

Hunters present: _____

Weather: _____

This is what happened:

_____

_____

_____

_____

_____

_____

_____

_____

_____

_____

_____

_____

_____

_____

_____

_____

Date: Hunting Location:

Hunters present:

Weather:

This is what happened:

Date: _____ Hunting Location: _____

_____

Hunters present: _____

_____

Weather: _____

This is what happened: _____

_____

_____

_____

_____

_____

_____

_____

_____

_____

_____

_____

_____

_____

_____

_____

_____

_____

If the memories you make
hunting are more important
than the kill you might
be a sportsman.
Go out in the woods,
get lost and find
yourself, or at least come
home with a deer.

Date: _____   Hunting Location: _____

_____

Hunters present: _____

_____

Weather: _____

This is what happened: _____

_____

_____

_____

_____

_____

_____

_____

_____

_____

_____

_____

_____

_____

_____

Date: _____ Hunting Location: _____

_____

Hunters present: _____

_____

Weather: _____

This is what happened: _____

_____

_____

_____

_____

_____

_____

_____

_____

_____

_____

_____

_____

_____

Date: _____ Hunting Location: _____

Hunters present: _____

Weather: _____

This is what happened: _____

_____

_____

_____

_____

_____

_____

_____

_____

_____

_____

_____

_____

_____

_____

_____

Date: Hunting Location:

Hunters present:

Weather:

This is what happened:

Date: _____ Hunting Location: _____

Hunters present: _____

Weather: _____

This is what happened: _____

_____

_____

_____

_____

_____

_____

_____

_____

_____

_____

_____

_____

_____

_____

Date: Hunting Location:

Hunters present:

Weather:

This is what happened:

Date: Hunting Location:

Hunters present:

Weather:

This is what happened:

Find your self and your game in the woods.

Date: Hunting Location:

Hunters present:

Weather:

This is what happened:

Date: Hunting Location:

Hunters present:

Weather:

This is what happened:

Date: Hunting Location:

Hunters present:

Weather:

This is what happened:

Date: Hunting Location:

Hunters present:

Weather:

This is what happened:

Date: Hunting Location:

Hunters present:

Weather:

This is what happened:

Live, Laugh, Hunt

Date: Hunting Location:

Hunters present:

Weather:

This is what happened:

Date: _____ **Hunting Location:** _____

Date: Hunting Location:

Hunters present:

Weather:

This is what happened:

Date: Hunting Location:

Hunters present:

Weather:

This is what happened:

Date: Hunting Location:

Hunters present:

Weather:

This is what happened:

Date: Hunting Location:

Hunters present:

Weather:

This is what happened:

Date: _____ Hunting Location: _____

Hunters present: _____

Weather: _____

This is what happened: _____

_____

_____

_____

_____

_____

_____

_____

_____

_____

_____

_____

_____

_____

_____

Go Hunt.

A hunting story:

As the story goes, about 40 years ago in Pennsylvania, on a snowy Christmas Day, my rather large family of cousins gathered together at my Grandmother's on Christmas afternoon. A holiday tradition, of families sharing Christmas Day, that has continued for over half of a century.(Thanks to my cousin Denny & Weesie and now their son Adam, who graciously opened their homes on Christmas Day).

My father, cousins, brothers and family friends who hunt, always had a good time during the season swapping stories about the deer harvest.

Of course, it was not without rivalry and jokes. The tales would go on and on. Who shot a deer, who got the biggest buck, who missed the biggest buck, who only got a doe, and who missed all the shots.

One year, when one of the cousins Johnny, missed a doe, my Dad gave him a hard time, teasing him and adding, "Oh, I could get one with a club if I had to."

The next year my father who stated he could kill a doe with a club, missed the doe and Johnny didn't. On Christmas Day, Johnny presented him a wrapped present, a piece of hickory, later known by all as Uncle Pete's Deer Club. As the club became passed back and forth a tradition was created. The club is now mounted on a board and my cousin Denny states, "It is the most feared present at Christmas time."

That hickory stick became a family tradition. Every Christmas for almost 40 years, our large extended family gathers together to hear the story of the club, and then watch as it is presented to some unlucky member of the family who missed a deer. There is a record book with a list of names of all who received Uncle Pete's Deer Club, and a list of rules, added over the years, to help determine the recipient.

A precious meaningful family tradition, a ritual that has been carried down for decades.

This is how traditions begin.

It is up to us, to create traditions and carry them on.

Inspire your group of hunters to start a tradition.

Keep a record of the hunts during the season.

Collect your memories.

The last pages of this book can be used to keep a yearly log of the hunters in your group or family.

Year   Hunter

Year	Hunter

Year   Hunter

Year   Hunter

Year	Hunter

Books With Soul

Books with Soul believes in sharing gifts that inspire and motivate
others to create memories and keep a record of the story of their life.

WE believe every life is worth a few written words to pass on or reflect on in the future.
You don't have to be an author to tell the story of your life. Just be you.
Today will be the good old days someday, remember them.
Thank you for becoming a Memory Collector.

Questions? Email info@bookswithsoul.com
We appreciate every reader, every traveler and recorder of history.
We would love if you took the time to write a
review on Amazon and let us know if the books motivated you.

Find more journals, inspiration, diaries, coloring books and gifts for every
milestone at
www.bookswithsoul.com

If you would like to have a personalized journal for
an organization, company,
group, club, family
or activity, contact
Books with Soul.
Special unique journals in 20 quantities or more can
be created.

*if someone bought you this journal, pay it forward and **buy a journal**
for someone
you care about.
Help them write the story of their life.

Other Books With Soul Journals:
Words I Want to Say
Every Breath- A Journal of Gratitude & Blessings
Crazy Ramblings of a Pregnant Woman
Remember When: Guest Book
Camp Memories
Reflections from the Beach
Pregnancy Journal: When We Were One
The Adventures of US
Reflections of My Year
I was here
Dirt Road Diaries: My off-road adventures
Seriously I'm 50?
Old Soul

Anniversary editions available on Amazon:
1st Anniversary: One Epic Year
5th Anniversary: Five Epic Years
10th Anniversary: Ten Epic Years
15th Anniversary: Fifteen Epic Years
20th Anniversary: Twenty Epic Years
25th Anniversary: Twenty-five Epic Years
30th Anniversary: Thirty Epic Years
35th Anniversary: Thirty-five Epic Years
40th Anniversary: Forty Epic Years
45th Anniversary: Forty-five Epic Years
50th Anniversary: Fifty Epic Years

Perfect Anniversary Gift

Books with Soul ™

was inspired from a lover of music and life, who believed in the soul.

He had a collection of wonderful things. Physical memories you could read, touch, and listen to- including thousands of vinyl albums.

Old school music, that lasts forever. In 2018, he passed away from brain cancer, but his memory lives on as others go old school. Collect pieces of your history, put pencil to paper, and record written memories.

A physical book will not be lost in the cloud, and will last longer than a lifetime.

Keep a record of the story of your life. Your Words. Your Pages.

This is for you Mark.

Bookswithsoul.com
Your Words. Your Pages.

Made in the USA
Las Vegas, NV
03 December 2023

82009946R00066